Jennifer
Much Love
Dolphin

D1520942

GOD, ARE YOU STILL THERE?

A Desperate Cry for Help Through Life's Struggles

Delphine Noble

In Honor of my Mother Easter Mae Noble

For all the times you were there for me, for all the
Godly wisdom that you imparted and all the
knowledge you shared

It took some time to understand the lessons that
you so willingly gave me---memories that will
never fade away

∞

To My Children: Candace, Yheme, Phetiema,
Nekia, Paul and Shardee ---Who were all with me
in my dark places

To my siblings who stood by me in the hard times
To my Pastor's L.T. Walker Jr. & Sandra Walker
who led me to Jesus Christ

…With my deepest love, I dedicate my testimony

Introduction

If you feel that you are trapped by life's circumstances and think there is no hope, or if you are wondering "God, are you still there?" then this book is for you!

I was inspired by God to write about things in my past to help people who think that there is no way out. Based on some things that I have gone through; I know that the Lord was always there. I am learning to enjoy my life because I now realize that God will never leave me. The great thing about it is that he is not a respecter of persons. What he did for me, he'll do for anyone who trusts and believes in him.

▪Chapter 1

Growing up in the country had its ups and downs. Some things I tried to forget, but I realized that there are things in my past that could help someone else. I was born in a small southern town and raised in a small community that we referred to as the *country*. Like most people in the country, we had our own garden. It was not like the gardens today, which are just a little of this and a little of that. We had just about everything: things like beans, greens, potatoes, berries, pears, and peaches, just to name a few. We also had animals; they were almost like part of the family (and I have a reason for saying *almost*). Bill was a racehorse. He belonged to a friend of the family, but he was trained on our property. It was always exciting to go for a ride. He was a tall, gray stallion, and he was so tall that we had to use a bucket to reach the saddle whenever we wanted to ride. And then there was Sparkey, our Shetland pony. He was beautiful. He had a long, flowing mane that we loved to brush. Our bull, Sukgersey, was sort of mean. We were not allowed to go inside the fence. My brother, John, would always take chances teasing him. One day, John had to outrun the bull. Sukgersey didn't catch him, but the barbed-wire fence did. I'm sure that was better than getting caught by the bull. Our cow's name was Ladybug. She was big but very gentle. We didn't have lots of animals, so most of them had names. But one day, it all came to an end. All of our pigs, hogs, and chickens—and even our animals with names—began to go to their final destinations: Bill got too old to race and was taken away; Sparkey was bitten by a snake and died; Ladybug and Sukgersey eventually went to my grandfather's smokehouse. I know that might sound a little harsh, but that was their purpose for living.

Even though we lived on a small farm, my father and mother worked very hard to get the things that we needed. We didn't have a lot, but we were happy. My dad worked on a few large farms. I will never forget the Hillmans. They helped me to realize that race was only a color, but under that color, we are all the same. My mother worked as a nurse aide. She worked with my friend's mother, so whenever she worked on Saturday, I would go to town and spend that day at her house.

We went to church a lot, and not just because we wanted to go. Don't get me wrong: I enjoyed going to church, but it just seemed as though we were there all the time. School, on the other hand, was a different story. I hated my elementary years. If you have ever been bullied, you know what I mean. It wasn't because I couldn't fight; I just didn't want to. But sometimes I had to fight just to survive. No one seemed to notice that I was being picked on, and for some odd reason, I just wouldn't tell. I have always been the type of person who takes things to heart, always wanting to be myself yet always wanting to fit in. It didn't matter who I had to become as long as I was accepted. Many times, I put my heart out there to be stepped on—and believe me, there are people who will walk all over you. When my feelings were hurt, my heart would hurt so much that I would become physically sick. On the other hand, whenever I was happy, it seemed as though my insides would explode with joy. I love to help people, and I know that's one of the gifts that God has given me. This is a gift that, if not used wisely, could cause serious pain.

I attended a small church in the country. I really enjoyed going to church. It was one place where I felt that I could fit in. Sunday school was my favorite. When the teacher was teaching, I would find myself daydreaming, and sometimes it almost felt like I was there. Our pastor was an awesome pastor and mentor. He treated everyone the same, and I felt that he really loved all of us. As a teenager, I could hardly wait to get to church to hear him preach. He was not a *hummer*, but I could listen to him teach all day. The sermon I remembered most as a young child was when he preached on speaking in tongues. I always thought that was something I wanted to do, not knowing what it really meant. It was just so captivating, and I wanted to know everything about it. I found myself praying to God for those tongues. It actually happened. I began to speak with other tongues in my teen years. This was great. I felt that God was about to do something special in my life. I knew that he always heard my prayers, but this was new to me, and I was very excited. Eventually, I started to feel different about the whole thing. It seemed as though I no longer had any friends. No one really wanted to be around me. It seemed that all my friends at the church were avoiding me. Whenever they would go out to eat or to a concert, I was left behind. I felt so alone that most of the time I just stayed to myself. I wanted to fit in so badly that I began to push myself away from speaking in tongues or even spending my regular time with God. From that point, I would always find myself just trying to fit in anywhere that I could fit. I allowed people to use me and take my kindness for weakness. I didn't want to be this person I had become, and it was making me angry.

I was almost always depressed when it was time to go to school because I knew that I would have to do things that I didn't want do—or get beat up. Some days, I went as far as to skip school. One time, someone saw me and told my mom, which was worse than getting beat up. This went on for years. I even began to pick on others who were younger than me. It made no sense at all! That's when I first realized that people who are hurting seem to hurt other people. I had planned to hurt so many people who had hurt me, and year after year, it was on my mind. My junior high years were much better. Most of the people who bullied me had dropped out of school, but I would still see them from time to time. The anger was still building in me. When I got to high school, it was so much better, but a lot of the anger was still there.

▪Chapter 2

May 18, 1980—I did it! I graduated from high school! Most of my thoughts of hurting people were gone. My high school years were good, and I continued to go to church—and no one made me go. I was enjoying growing up. I decided to go to a vocational school in another small town, not far from where I lived. There were people of different ages and backgrounds, and I was doing something that I really wanted to do. I made lots of friends, and I received my certificate in business administration. After graduation, I went up north to spend time with my relatives and to see if that was where I wanted to live. It was the biggest place I had ever seen! Surrounded by uncles, aunties, and cousins, I should have felt right at home. It was so different from the country! After about six months, I decided that it just wasn't my cup of tea—green tea was not popular at that time, and I was definitely green! So, I returned home, wondering what I was going to do next.

My sister Grace lived in Boston, and she wanted me to stay with her for a while, but I never considered living there. Later, my brother-in-law passed away, and Grace moved back to town. She was eight or nine months pregnant. I figured maybe I could handle moving to town.

Another sister, Maud, and I shared a nice apartment with her, and we got along great. After my niece was born, Grace wanted to move to the country. I never thought that would happen. Going to church and visiting my mother was fine but moving back was out of the question. Well, I found myself back in the country. My best friend, Beverly, moved with us. Four grown women and a baby all under one roof, and we still got along great! That was a miracle in itself. The house that we moved into was so beautiful. It was a three-bedroom home with a huge dining room and living room, and it had the most beautiful fireplace I had ever seen. This house sat right beside the lake. I was so happy for Grace because she deserved something as nice as this. Shortly after we were settled, I noticed that we always had company. Her friends would always need something, and it was always an emergency. My sister had many close friends during this time. I thought they were coming over to see the baby or our Beautiful home. Later, I found out that my sister had received a large amount of money after her husband's death. She became a lender to lots of people, but they didn't intend to pay her back. I don't remember her getting mad at them. Time went on, and the parties, barbeques, volleyball games, and other events kept going on until one day, we had to move. All those "friends" who borrowed did nothing to help. I learned that sometimes people don't always intend to hurt you, but it can end up that way. Eventually, we got past that, and life went on. Beverly moved to Detroit; Maud got married; Grace and my niece and I moved back to town. I had no clue what to do with my life at that point. I would go to church because that's what I was taught to do, but I felt that there was a big world out there, and I wanted to be part of it. So that's what I did. I decided to go to the Job Corp. I had a close male friend, and I thought he would be happy for me when I told him that I was leaving—but he cried! I had no idea we were that close. Even though I had feelings for him, I never let it show. I knew he wanted to be a preacher, and I saw no room for me. I left anyway because I thought I needed to find myself—mistake!

Oklahoma wasn't as big as Illinois, but it was bigger than the country and town. I was excited and nervous. I knew nobody, but I wouldn't turn back. I met lots of people from different places and was so amazed at the lifestyles of people who I thought were just like me. I began to realize that we are all different. While I was in the big O, I went to school to study electronics. Unfortunately, I was not interested in it, and I threw that right out of the window. I lived in a dorm with about twenty other young ladies. It was a co-ed dorm, so there were young men downstairs. Most of them were very young and immature. There were two guys who would always follow me around: one was white and the other one was an Indian (race has never mattered to me when it came to friendship). They were true friends. I got along with just about everyone, so I thought this had to be the place for me.

I started to date at the age of twenty-one. I was considered an old maid, but I wish I had waited longer. There was no one on campus that I was interested in, so I decided to look elsewhere. I met a few men, but at that time, I thought it was useless. There are some strange people out there! I decided to go out with my friend, and to my surprise, she had invited a date for me! I remember being mad at her because he was nothing to look at, and I could not believe he was only after one thing! That ended right away. He came around the dorm looking for me, but I was never anywhere to be found, so I guess he gave up. Later, I met a very handsome, intelligent, absolutely perfect young man—so I thought. He was a little younger than I preferred, but he was more than handsome—he was gorgeous! Needless to say, it wasn't long before I was trying to mend my heart. I cried a lot after finding out that he had moved to Texas. I finally realized that he was not coming back, and I moved on. I threw myself back into reality. I went back to class and started to hang out with my friends again.

One day I noticed this guy hanging around the dorm. He kept following my friends and I— that was a bold man. He was flirting a lot, and it had started to get on my nerves because I could still remember picking up the pieces of a broken heart. This went on for a while. He refused to leave me alone, so I agreed to let him take me out. His name was Harold. He was a charmer and a real gentleman. We went out a couple of times: downtown to the mall, to the ice-skating rink, and to a few restaurants. Before I knew what had happened, I had fallen again. I started to go to his house on weekends. Sometimes I wouldn't make it back on time, and my pass would be revoked for the next weekend. I thought I was having the time of my life. I had started to get sick, so I went to see the school nurse. I thought that my heart would fail me when she told me that I was pregnant. How would I tell Harold? Would he stay with me? So many questions ran through my mind at once. I knew I had to tell him, but how? I had no choice but to just do it. We were happy, yet in shock, not knowing what we were going to do. I could tell by the look in his eyes that he was not ready. My heart had never been so crushed.

I called my mom, explained the situation, and asked if I could come home. She welcomed me back with open arms. Who could ask for a more loving mother?

Harold wanted me to stay, but neither of us knew where we would go from that point. Being aware that I knew no one, I decided to leave. We even went to visit his mother, and she seemed to be happy about the baby, but, still unsure of what to do, I returned home.

I moved in with my sister Grace. She seemed so happy to have me back. When my beautiful baby girl was born, I moved to the country with my sister Gloria. She lived right next door to my mom. I talked with Harold once more after leaving Oklahoma. At that time, we talked about getting back together and raising our daughter, but for some reason, that was our last conversation. It was as though he had fallen off the face of the earth. I had no idea what happened to him. Months passed, and I decided to move back to town.

▪Chapter 3

This time, I wanted my own home. I moved to an apartment. It was so peaceful there. This was something I had accomplished, and I was enjoying every minute of it. Just me and my baby, Candace! My sister Gloria would come and get her often, so it was mostly just me. I still went to church in the country because there was just something about the pastor's teaching that kept me going back. I got a job at a clothing store in town. I really wanted to be independent, and that was a start. I didn't have a car, so I walked a lot.

After a few weeks of just working, sleeping, and going to church, I felt that I had a boring life, and I had to do something. I decided to go to the club. In a short time, I had quit my job and begun to party more and more. I felt that it was time to have someone in my life. I talked to a couple of guys, but I knew them, and I wouldn't even attempt to make it work. One night, I met Danny. We talked and went out for a short time before we started to play house. The peace was gone, and there was so much frustration in my life, but yet I felt I needed someone. And by this time, he had me thinking he was the only one. He did a little here and there, but we never discussed marriage. Although marriage meant a lot to me at the time, I wouldn't dare talk about it in fear that I would be alone once again.

Danny was partying a lot more than I was at this time. Whatever was mine was his, and whatever was his was his. Every time I went to my closet, I saw he had brought a few more things, and without even asking, he was living in my house. I didn't know what was going on. I was not scared of him, so I could have very easily put him out. It was as though my mouth was wired shut. Even when I disagreed, somehow, I agreed.

There were people all around me with whom I would associate from time to time. My cousin Wimberly and his wife, Carolyn, lived upstairs. Carolyn was great when I needed someone to talk to. Sometimes we would talk for hours while cooking dinner and planning for an occasional weekend out. My cousin Joyce, who lived in the apartment complex as well, was always there for me. If I had taken some of her advice, I wouldn't have been in the situation that I was. She had identical twin girls and a son. I always thought she had her hands full. After only a few months in my own apartment, I found out that I was pregnant again. I appreciated Joyce more than ever. She even went with me to my four-month checkup. I was so big; she would always say that I might be having twins. She gave me the moral support that Danny should have given me, but I was just thankful that someone was there. It was almost over. The doctor wanted to listen to the baby's heartbeat. It was healthy. But then he heard another healthy heartbeat! That's right; I was having twins! It's a good thing I was lying down. It was a long three months.

They were born two months early, small but healthy. I had to leave them in the hospital for a few days, but Yheme and Phetiema were real troopers. I had three babies under five years old. I remember crying many nights because I thought I couldn't do it, but I made it one day at a time. I stayed home a lot—alone. Every now and then, I would get a break. Danny would find it in his heart to be there on occasions and, of course, I would let him. Somehow, I found myself back in the country with my sister. This time, we lived in a trailer. It was peaceful most of the time. I really enjoyed it, but I wanted my own place, and I was determined to get it.

About a year later, I was missing something. I can almost feel the knot that was in my throat as I thought about having not three, but four children under five with no home of my own. One minute I was thinking, "I can't wait to grow up," and now this! I loved all of my children, and there had to be a way to make this work. Danny and I were still fighting about him being gone so much, and I felt so alone. Even though we wouldn't dare live together in my sister's house, I felt as though he should have been around to help out.

A few months later, my daughter, Nekia, was born. I knew that it was time to find my own place. Danny suggested that we move up north and make a fresh start. Frightened and confused, I agreed to move to Milwaukee.

▪Chapter 4

I began to make arrangements before I could change my mind. I called Doris, my nephew's mother, the only person I knew in Milwaukee at that time. Later, I realized that I had another friend there, Chris (she was adopted into the family as my sister, and we treated her no different). Doris was so happy that I was coming. Now my baby was two months old, and I could wait no longer. I packed and was on my way: my baby and me. The other children would come with their father after I found a place to stay. Doris invited us to stay with her until I got settled. I stayed with her for a short time before finding a place of my own. The apartment was perfect. It had two bedrooms, but my children were small, so that was okay. The kitchen was what I liked most because the oven was built into the wall. You wouldn't find that in my neighborhood down south. My children finally arrived, and I was so glad to see them. The first few weeks were great … and then, my dream started to turn into a nightmare! I found myself yelling at my children a lot. I was so stressed! Danny stayed out later and later. Sometimes he would come in the next day. He would always apologize after the argument and promise never to do it again. Of course, I would always forgive him. What choice did I have?

I think he really got tired of running and staying out late, so one night when the children were asleep, he introduced me to someone he had been hanging out with. Her name was Cocaine. That was the start of my nightmare. He said that it wouldn't hurt me and that it was a really good high. I had never heard of the stuff before, but after all, if it was better than weed, I was willing to give it a try. I never really cared for the blunt or even the joint. It made me sick. I just did it to fit in. He showed me how to cook the cocaine, and he fussed at me for cooking it wrong. Then he would show me how to smoke it and fussed at me for smoking it wrong. I was thinking how stupid the whole thing was! If he had known how much I flushed down the toilet, I would not be here to tell the story. This continued for months, and I was so frustrated with him that I made myself learn to cook and smoke it. My pillow stayed full of tears after that day. We went to the welfare office to sign up for food stamps and a check. I was shocked when the caseworker told me that I would get over six hundred dollars cash and so many food stamps that I didn't know what to buy first! I was so excited—that is until I got home.

Danny's habit was a lot bigger than mine at that time, so he could not resist the thought of buying drugs. Somehow we managed to buy beds for the children and furniture for our apartment, thanks to Doris, who made sure that I had transportation to get the things I needed. I tried so hard to hide the money that we needed to pay our rent, but most of the time it didn't work. The landlord started to come by several times a month to collect the rent until one day, I had nothing to give him. This went on for months. Sometimes I would give him just enough to keep a roof over our heads. Even the food started to get low because I would have to sell some of our food stamps to keep up with other bills. One day, I told Danny that I was going to the store. He knew that I didn't have any money, but he didn't try to stop me. Knowing that I was going to do the wrong thing, I started to pray. I don't even remember what I prayed. I had three long blocks to change my mind, but I needed to get something for us to eat. I tried to talk myself out of it all the way to the store, but my stomach wouldn't let me.

When I got there, I walked up and down every aisle. Finally, I picked up a few things. Instead of just getting something to eat, I saw a few more things that we needed, so I got them too. That's when I decided that I had better get out of there. I walked right past the register and almost out the door when someone stopped me. It was an undercover security guard. He asked me to walk with him to the back of the store. He had been watching me the whole time. While waiting for the police to arrive, we had a couple of cigarettes and talked about how I had gotten myself into this mess. He said that if I had let him know that I only wanted food, he wouldn't have called the police. When everything was over, I left with a ticket. My heart was still beating out of control, and I must have smoked three cigarettes before I got home. Danny was glad that I didn't go to jail, probably because he had the kids. I knew I had to get food, and that's when I found out about food pantries. It was up to me once again to get out and Beat the streets to get food on the table. Now we had plenty of food, but the rent was still due.

When I got my first eviction notice, I knew it was time to pack. After about a month of dodging the landlord, we had a visit from the sheriff. We managed to put a lot of things in our neighbor's basement. I knew that they were Christians, and they really showed us love that day. They offered us food and even let us stay at their apartment for a few hours. Pride (and Danny) kept me from telling them that we had nowhere to go. Danny went down the street and returned in a few hours and said that he had found us a temporary place to stay. It would keep us off the street, at least for the night. I packed a few things, as much as we could carry, and we walked down the street. The nightmare grew worse! As we walked up the stairs of this old, shabby, abandoned apartment, I wanted to cry. There I was with my four babies—under five years old—living here in a dope house! I didn't know how long we would be there or if the police would show up and take my children. There were a few pieces of furniture, and the house was on its last leg. There were a couple of mattresses on the floor that I was scared to let my children sleep on. The children were really tired and cranky, and I was craving a hit. That's when I realized I was an addict. Danny and I talked later that night, and he informed me that since we didn't have any money to pay them, that I would have to babysit their kids. Not while they worked, but whenever they would go out and find drugs and smoke in the next room—all night! (It was shocking enough to find out that there were other kids in this mess!) Whenever they thought I was really mad, they would give me a hit to calm me down. I don't remember how long we were there, but it seemed like years. I decided that I couldn't take it another minute!

Danny found another friend who I was almost afraid to meet, but I knew that it would be hard to find something worse than where we already were. He was neatly dressed and seemed to be okay. His name was Clyde. He talked to his wife, and she asked us to come over. Thank God! We were in a clean apartment with beds and a shower! I remember thanking God as we got cleaned up. I just couldn't seem to be able to resist the cold beer that was offered, even though I knew the craving for cocaine would be at a high. They had two children just about the same age as mine. There were only two bedrooms in the apartment, but they made room for us. Cheryl invited me onto a small balcony outside of their bedroom. We barbequed, laughed, cried, and got totally wasted that night. That quickly, I forgot how hard I had prayed for God's help and began to party again. Yet, Clyde and Cheryl seemed to be our ticket out. I called my mom and pretended that everything had been going okay. I told her that we had lost our apartment, and we were staying with friends, but there was no way I could tell her what had happened in between. My children seemed to be so happy. I'm sure that the warm bath and sleeping in a nice, clean bed again helped out a lot. We slept well that night. Even though I didn't give up the habits, God let me live—and learn!

I eventually got in touch with Doris to let her know everything was okay. I eventually got in touch with Chris. She let everyone know that I was her sister. She made sure I kept in touch. From this point, it seemed that everything was going my way. Cheryl and I partied, and welfare took care of our children. I even rented an apartment in the building we were living in. The blessings were pouring in, and I was still doing my thing. Candace, my oldest, went to stay with my mom for a while. Once again, I was missing something. No, not again! I was really scared this time because I was drinking and even smoking a little cocaine. Milwaukee County had no tolerance for drugs in the baby's system. I cried and thought about my baby a lot. I thought that if I went to get help, they would take my other children. Months went by, and I smoked less and less, but the fact remained that I had drugs in my system. I was scared! I stopped completely for a while. I went into the hospital and had my baby, Shardee, alone, but I was determined to take care of my children. My baby was clean, and so was I. That was a miracle. After being released from the hospital, I returned to my habit.

▪Chapter 5

God knows I wanted to change, but for some strange reason, I didn't know how. Things were a little better because we had a roof over our heads, and we were a family. Candace was still with my mother in Arkansas, and though I missed her every day, I knew that she would be okay. Our food was just about gone, and I knew it was a long time before I would get food stamps, so I went to the local food bank. It was very full that month. I met an older lady, Ms. Cora, and we talked while we waited in line. She really seemed to understand what I was going through. She gave me her address and invited me to come over to her house whenever I needed to talk. She said that she had powdered milk that I could have to stretch my food. I didn't think city people knew anything about powdered milk. It was a short time later when I was out of milk and remembered Ms. Cora. My baby, Shardee, was five weeks old that day; it was February 14, 1989—Valentine's Day. He looked at me and smiled for the very first time. I can see that smile to this day.

I called my newfound friend to see if the offer was still on for the milk. She lived about five or six blocks away. It had started to snow, so I bundled up, kissed my babies, and headed out the door. I thought I would never get there. It was cold, but I was glad to get out of the house. She was glad to see me, and to my surprise, she offered me a beer. Danny was always good with kids when he was around, so I decided to sit and talk for a minute. This would be a good Valentine's Day gift. The time had gone by very fast. Just as I was about to leave, the phone started to ring. I could hear Danny's voice on the other end. It sent chills down my spine. When she handed me the phone, my heart was already racing. I can still hear the words he said to me: "Shardee is not breathing. I gave him his bottle, laid him down, went back to check on him, and he's not breathing. I think he's dead." At that point, I almost fell to my knees, but I knew I had to get home. I don't remember how I explained to Ms. Cora at the time, but I left running. The snow was deep now, almost halfway my calves. This made it hard for me to run, but it didn't stop me. I was crying and praying as I ran all the way home. The five blocks seemed like ten. I made it home, and Danny was standing in the doorway with Shardee, limp, in his hands. I remember seeing his little feet and hands turning blue before my eyes. I took my baby gently, held him close, and began to cry even more while still gasping for breath. I asked Danny if he had called anyone else, and he was shaking his head no. I put Shardee in his crib and ran to the phone and dialed 911. I ran violently up the stairs to Cheryl and Clyde's apartment, screaming for them to help me. Cheryl met me at the door, trying to figure out what was going on. I don't remember losing consciousness, but the next thing I remember, I was back in my apartment, trying to answer questions from the ambulance attendants. I don't even remember hearing the sirens. They kept working on my baby, but I knew that he was gone. His small-framed, lifeless body was just there with no sign of life.

The next thing I remember was talking to the doctor. I don't even remember everything we talked about until he asked me if I wanted to hold my baby. I held him and kissed him. I did not want to give him back. To some people, this might sound a little weird, but this was my baby. It seemed as though my heart was being ripped out. I was numb. Parts of my life kept jumping around as though I were in a movie, and the scenes were going by really fast. Now I was in the car with two women police officers on my way back home. They were trying to keep me calm, so there were periods of silence. All of a sudden, the silence was broken by one of the officers apologizing for the action they were about to take. That's when I realized that I had missed part of a very important conversation. And then I heard, "I'm sorry they have to take your children away." At that moment, my emotions were out of control. I think it would have been better for them to shoot me. They were shocked that no one had told me. We all started to cry at this point. It was as if it were their children too.

When we pulled up in front of the apartment, two social workers met me and told me that they were there to pick up my children. There was no sympathy. They walked in with me and started to take my children. I was trying to find out what was going on, but they insisted that I get them a few clothes and diapers, and they started to walk out. My babies cried and reached for me. I could no longer keep my composure. I tried to kiss them and tell them everything would be all right, but the tears would not stop coming. As they pulled off, I could see my babies crying and still reaching for me. Cheryl was trying to talk to me, but at this point, I could no longer hear what anyone was saying. I don't remember if I passed out, but later I found myself standing beside Shardee's crib. Danny was trying to talk to me, but I couldn't figure out why my baby was dead, my other children were taken away, and I was so alone. I kept seeing Shardee smiling at me. The very first smile he gave me, and the last. I couldn't help thinking that maybe he was saying goodbye. That night, I ran into his bedroom several times and looked into his bed, where I knew I heard him crying. I kept wishing it was a bad nightmare, and I would find him sleeping in his crib. But it didn't happen; he was not there.

Cheryl talked me into giving the crib to the Red Cross, hoping it would help me get some sleep, but that didn't help. Danny kept going over the story about how Shardee died. It was driving me crazy. The police had informed us that we wouldn't get our children back until the investigation was over. I couldn't believe they would even think we had anything to do with our baby's death. I knew that if I just told the truth, everything would be over and I would get my children back.

A few days later, there was one of Milwaukee's most popular anchormen standing right at my door. When I saw the camera crew with him, I absolutely refused to be on television. He assured me that he would not put me on air, and he only wanted my story about what had happened. I believed everything was on the ups, so I relaxed and answered the questions that he asked me. I told him everything that I knew, which was mostly what Danny had told me. He seemed to be very sympathetic, and they were gone. I ran upstairs and told Cheryl what had happened. She didn't think it was a good idea since the investigation was going on. I still thought everything would be okay because I had nothing to hide. That night, I heard my voice on TV. I was on the news! They didn't show my face, but everything I said was on tape. I could only cry. He had tricked me. A couple of days later, the police came and took us to the police station for questioning. It was as though they were accusing us of doing something wrong. Danny and I started out talking to the police officers together. Later, Danny was taken to another room. I found myself sitting in the room alone. The officer came back and told me that I could leave. As we walked down the hall, I started to look for Danny. I was just about to ask where he was when I saw him passing with another officer. He was wearing handcuffs! My knees started to buckle, and my stomach was in knots. The officer was trying to explain to me that he was being arrested for second-degree reckless homicide, but that meant nothing to me at this point. I started to get sick as I cursed at him, trying to find out what was going on. He only hung his head and walked with the officer. Right then, my life seemed to come to an end. I went into my empty apartment and cried.

Chapter 6

My life was a mess, and I couldn't see it getting any better. I slowly walked upstairs to let Clyde and Cheryl know what was happening. Everything seemed to run through my mind. I wondered what my baby had gone through: Did he cry out to me? Did he wonder what was happening to him? The pain had overtaken his tiny body, and I wasn't there! I finally came to myself enough to call my mom and dad. If it wasn't for my mother, I don't know what would have happened next. Within a few days, my mother was there, and I had never been happier to see her. My sister Gloria, my brother Tim, and my cousin Clint, Jr came with her. I really wanted to see Candace, but I understood why my mom did not bring her. I felt a lot better, but I knew that the worst was yet to come.

My apartment was empty and cold. My mother and sister helped me write the obituary. I looked at his picture a lot, and sometimes it was as if he were right there with me. If I could have gone back to that morning, he smiled at me; I would have stayed home. I couldn't even begin to count how many packs of cigarettes I smoked since this was the saddest day of my life. My throat was sore from smoking so much, but I would not let myself feel any pain. My mother was so concerned. In just a few days, my welfare grant had gone from over eight hundred dollars to nothing. The government quickly let me know that they would no longer help me because I had no dependents. I had to get a job. My mother stayed around as long as I needed her, and I really needed her. The funeral home attendant asked if I wanted to dress my baby. When we got there, I just couldn't do it. That's when I saw my baby's head had been cut from his forehead to the back of his neck. I felt my self getting sick. I never thought they would have to do an autopsy. My mother dressed him while I stood outside the room.

Now it was time for the hardest day of my life. As we were getting dressed for the funeral, I whispered to my mom that I couldn't do it. She tried to explain to me why this was something I had to do. As I approached the funeral home, my knees got weak, and I was about to faint. Tim and Clint, Jr helped me to my seat. The small box did not look big enough for Shardee. For some reason, I thought he needed air. There were some weird thoughts going through my mind that I seemed to have no control over. I don't remember the sermon because I knew what was coming next. I really begin to panic as I thought about the cemetery. I remember telling my mom that I knew

I could not make it through this. As we pulled up to the gravesite, I felt faint again. A prayer was said by my brother-in-law, Oscar, and they begin to bury the casket. I felt a knot in my stomach that I had never felt before and then a cry that hurt my heart so much I thought that I would never recover. *He can't breathe*, I thought, and the tears would not stop. I don't even remember when I stopped crying.

For a few days, I was what you would call a zombie. Thank God that my mom was there to help me through those first few days. Eventually, I had to let her get back home. Now I was hurting to see my children. Candace was still down south, and my other children were scattered over the city, and I had no idea where. I had to make arrangements to see my children, which seemed to take forever. It took a few weeks, but I was so excited when they finally let me see them. Nekia, my two-year-old, had been placed with a lady who had no idea how to take care of her, even though she was wealthy and traveled a lot. The worker informed me that she had asked to take her out of the country (on vacation), but there was no way I could agree to that. When I saw her, I cried. They told me that the lady was really a good person, but I could tell that she had no idea how to take care of a black baby. Nekia was as white as snow. I guess that was from not using a lotion on her skin.

Her hair was so dry that I thought it would break when I combed it. The social worker brought me whatever I needed to take care of her for that moment. But first, I just hugged her and cried with joy. Yheme and Phetiema were in the next room. When I saw them, I could only cry more. They were okay, but they looked so sad. As I picked them up and hugged them, I noticed that Phetiema's head would not stop shaking. It was as though she had a nervous condition. I seriously thought about running off with them, but Candace was not there, and I knew that I could not see her. So, I started to cry all over again. I felt that I was being punished for something when I had done nothing. The hours went by so fast, and I was alone again. The courts informed me that I would have to get a place to live and undergo a psychiatric evaluation. They probably thought I was slipping at this point. I thought they were crazy! The psychiatrist was outside Milwaukee (a suburban area). It was a Beautiful place, but I had no idea what I was about to get into. I was really nervous the first time. When I got there, I realized that I had no cigarettes, which left me thinking I could not make it through the session. After a few minutes with the psychiatrist, cigarettes were the least of my worries.

She was a little older than I thought a psychiatrist should be; nonetheless, she was the one who would hear my problems, and she had an ample supply of cigarettes! I started from the beginning. The room was fogged with our cigarette smoke. You see, she was a real smoker, and she supplied me with more cigarettes than I could smoke. The more I talked, the more we smoked. All of a sudden, she spoke. There was a lot of anger in her voice. For a moment, I thought she was angrier than I was. Her cursing interrupted me several times. We were in deep conversation when I realized that she was trying to talk me into committing murder. I really don't know if she even realized what she had said, but as I stared at the serious look on her face, she told me that they would probably not do anything to me, not even jail time; I found my thoughts connecting with hers, and I knew that it was time to go. After talking to Cheryl, I did realize that I would go to jail. I had to get my children back, so I continued each session and tried to tune her out. My anger was getting worse because now I had no one to talk to about what I was going through. She prescribed something for me to sleep, but I ended up selling most of it so that I could smoke something that kept me awake. Yes, my habit was at a new high. Whenever I left her office, I wondered what if I could kill Danny and actually get away with it as she said. I had to get that out of my head because God knows that I never wanted to go through anything like this again. I thought I could have been in prison at that time and not felt any worse. I was so glad when the last session was over. I could hardly wait to get out of there! The bus was packed that day, so I slowly headed for the back. It was really strange, but I could feel someone watching me. As I looked up, it felt as though someone put a knife in my stomach! There I was, standing face to face with Danny! What were the odds!

So many things began to run through my mind at once. I turned and ran to the front, telling the driver to stop the bus. I don't remember if I was scared that I would do something to him or that he would do something to me, but anger was still gripping my heart. He never followed me, but I could feel him watching as the bus pulled off. I was about twenty blocks from home. I cried and talked to myself and God. I really didn't know if God even heard me anymore. I felt that I was losing my mind. It seemed as though it took days to get home. At that time, I knew I needed help, but I felt that there was nowhere to go and nobody to turn to. I prayed as I usually did whenever I was in trouble, but now nothing made sense anymore. I wondered why Danny didn't say anything to me—was he up to something, or was he just as confused as I was? Everyone was apologizing for not letting me know in advance that he was being released, but it no longer mattered because it didn't help me sleep any better at night.

I remember drinking every night before I went to bed, and in the morning I would start all over again. Some nights, I would not even go to bed because I would always find the money for a hit. My drug habit was getting so bad that I didn't see myself keeping a job long enough to get my own place. I began to hang out with the wrong crowd, and things got even worse. The social workers were trying so hard to get my children in one home, but it just didn't happen. They told me that the only way would be to place them with a relative. But my relatives were down south. My children were put in custody of my sister Grace in Arkansas. I felt better that they were all together, but now I was really alone, and I didn't know how I could deal with that. I finally got clean enough to find a job, and I thought that this would be my turning point. Everything was going okay for a while, but I just didn't want to be alone. There was this one guy at my job who caught my eye. He was always flirting with me, so I decided to go out with him. His name was Paul. We partied a lot, and he was a good company. I never really thought about the consequences. I just didn't want to be alone. I started to go to his house and stay a couple of days at a time. One day Cheryl got really mad at me because she thought that I should have let her know where I was going. When I went back, she would not let me in the apartment. The next time I came with the police. She told them that I didn't come back, so she put all my things out. Everything I had was gone. All of my clothes, my baby's death certificate, even his baby picture—the only one I had. Now the only memories I had of Shardee were in my head or in the obituary. At this point, I really wanted to give up.

▪Chapter 7

I began to lose myself in the pipe. I still didn't know exactly what I was doing, but eventually, I learned. Along with drinking, the drug was my breakfast and dinner. I don't even know how I could afford it; it just kept coming. I tried to sell a little weed to help support the habit I had created, but it didn't work. I managed to get some clothes and personal items. And there I was with a habit and no job. I stayed with Paul for a while. In between getting high, I thought we had something special. He would listen to my problems, and he held me when I cried.

I began to get sick a lot, and I didn't even have to go to the doctor to know what was going on. Paul was concerned enough to make me put the pipe down. Now I was very scared, but at the same time, I was happy. Now I had someone with me. I had someone to talk to and to love. Even though I missed all of my children, I would have one of them with me right then. I moved in with my sister Chris. I was still alone and hurt because Paul and I were not together. My self-esteem was at rock bottom, and I felt that I just had to get away. My sister sent me a bus ticket, and I was on my way south. I had no intention of moving; I just wanted to see my children and feel that someone really cared. I had many dreams, but none of them would come true. I made it to Arkansas, and for a while, it seemed to be working out fine. I stayed with my mom in the country for a while. I decided I would let Paul know that I had decided to stay until the baby was born. He wasn't very happy since it would be for four months. It really didn't matter what he thought at that time because we were not together. Finally, I was clean and feeling good about myself. It took a lot of pain getting to that point, so I was enjoying that life.

I spent lots of time with Candace, along with the rest of my babies. I visited my friend, Lillie. I was so excited to find out she was pregnant too. It had been years since I'd seen her, but she hadn't changed. We talked and decided that we should do something to better ourselves while we waited. It was nursing school. This was something different for me, but it wouldn't hurt to try. We traveled to Pine Bluff every day to go to school. It relieved lots of tension, and I had lots of time to spend with my children. We both got our certificates (Lillie continued her career in nursing, but I decided it wasn't for me).

Now my baby was due. The time had gone by so fast that I was able to suppress some of the pain that I had gone through in Milwaukee, even though I thought about Shardee almost every night. It was Christmas Day, 1989, and I was in pain—I mean real pain. I decided to have my baby in Arkansas, where the rest of my children were born—all except Shardee. The pains got closer, and I was on my way. But when I saw the doctor, it was a different story. First I had to go to the mall and walk—that didn't work. After a few hours of pain, I was informed that he was turned the wrong way, and I couldn't deliver. That meant surgery.

This was scary. I had never had surgery for anything. I had heard that some people don't make it through surgery, so I was really stressed. I was having an epidural, and I overheard the doctor say that it was his first time administering it. My whole body started to shake uncontrollably. The doctor wasn't able to give me the shot after that, so they had to put me under. Of course, they woke me up to see my baby, and I was out again. I was so happy when it was all over, and I had a healthy baby boy—again. Now it was time to decide when and if I was going back to Milwaukee. The days seemed to get longer because I could not see myself leaving my children. I decided that I had to go back for so many reasons. But I knew that we would all be together soon. The bus ride was long, but Paul, Jr. slept almost all of the way, and I cried. Every day I talked to my baby and missed my other children.

A few days went by, and I received a call from the social worker. Just when I thought things couldn't get worse. It was time to go back to court to see what progress was made concerning my case. The judge seemed to be upset by the fact that I had had another baby so soon. I thought that the social worker did a great job explaining things, but the judge had the last say so. It was suggested and so ordered that my baby was to be placed with my other children until I was able to get a home that was appropriate for my family. At this point, I just wanted to die! I could not believe they were taking the only person that was holding it together for me. I tried to talk myself into moving back to Arkansas, but I would think about Shardee. My addiction also played a big part in my decision because now I felt myself wanting a hit. Many thoughts went through my head about just taking my kids and hiding out, but I knew it would never work. My sister took him in with the rest of my children, and now things began to get worse. I started to drink and smoke again, and it wasn't any better; it grew worse. I was so confused and lonely. Paul Jr. and I had stayed with his dad up until now.

I decided that since I didn't have my baby, I should go back and stay with Chris. She had no idea that I was smoking cocaine, and I did everything in my power to hide it from her. In order to hide it, I had to find something that she liked to do. Tiny's Lounge was right next door and we did love clubbing. Almost every night, we would be at the bar (and sometimes during the day). Almost everyone in the club would feel sorry for me and buy us drinks. Sometimes we would get started before noon. A few days out of the week, Paul would come to get me, and we would go to his house and do our thing so that Chris would never know. Somehow I was drawn to people who would just give me things that I knew I should not have. Many times I was shocked to find myself still alive the next morning. I dated a lot, but I didn't sleep with a lot of men. It was worse! Most of the men that I dated only wanted a partner to get high with. That was something I chose to do to numb myself from the pain that I felt. And I stayed high most of the time.

Eventually, I developed bronchial asthma. I would often go to the emergency room because sometimes I would smoke crack and find myself smoking two or three packs of cigarettes in one night. It would take all night to get my lungs clear enough to go home. That was a good feeling, but by the time I got out of the hospital, I had to have another cigarette. I was always thinking about finding a job and getting my kids back, but I thought I needed the drinking and smoking to keep me from thinking about what was going on in my life. I didn't realize I was making things so much worse. Every now and then, I would go to a temporary job service to look for work. It was a hard road, but I finally got a job, and it lasted for a while. I worked hard and enjoyed my job, but the habit I had was much stronger than my will to fight it. I worked as long and hard as I could, but it was mostly just supporting my habit. The drugs were taking over my life, and there seemed to be nothing I could do about it. It wasn't long before I was no longer able to go back to this job because I was too tired to get up, or I was still up. I was so scared, but I could only think of getting another hit.

At this point, I didn't really care. Yet a few minutes later, I knew it would be hours before I would stop crying. Shortly, the money was gone, and I couldn't think of anyone to go to for the next fix, so I had no choice but to think. I cried and prayed to God for hours to help me out of the hole that I was in, and I was shocked when He did just that. I sobered up long enough to finally get a job. Even though Paul was one of my supervisors, I decided that it was a job, and whether I liked it or not, I had to have that job. We got along well enough to work together, but every time I turned around, there he was, watching me. It was an easy job, so I learned to deal with it. I worked nights, so I would find myself partying all day. This left me feeling drained all week, looking forward to the weekend so that I could rest. After a few weeks, I realized that I was working to party, and I still had no money. When I realized that I was not getting anywhere, and Paul was getting on my last nerve, I quit. Now I was back to square one.

Things were worse now. I had no job, no money, no children—no life. All this time, I kept praying. Not once did I stop to think how displeasing the things that I was doing were to God. I just knew He would answer, but I realized that He didn't have to. The answer did come. Chris suggested that I should go to a shelter. I didn't know much about shelters, but what if it could hurt? I made the call, and they informed me within a few days that they would help. I packed an overnight bag and went to live with people that I had never seen before. I was there for a week, but it seemed like months. I had to do chores and even watch someone else's children. There was no drinking or drugs. The first few days, I thought I would die. I could not believe I stayed. But for some strange reason, every time I thought about leaving, someone was there to talk me out of it. Just talking about my children gave me the motivation to try harder. I knew that trying to raise five small children was going to be hard, but I couldn't imagine being without them much longer.

▪Chapter 8

I did it! A week without drinking or drugs. I felt like a new person. I wish I had put the cigarettes down too. We had a meeting to find out the size of the house or apartment I would need. They actually took for me house hunting, and we found a duplex the same day. They also paid my first month's rent and deposit, and let me stay there a few more days, which would give me enough time to get a job. Since I was clean, I didn't have a problem getting a job. Yet I decided not to go back to work at that time. I got my children back that month. It was really hard to get started, so I went on welfare. I received enough assistance to do everything that I needed to do. I did not forget to thank God. I stayed in touch with Paul during this time, so he did come over to help. I just never realized that I was still weak. Before I could settle in, I met my neighbors. It only took a couple of beers. By this time, looking for a job was no longer on my mind. I did keep in mind that I had a baby now, so most of the time I would do what I had to do. I always bought my children what I thought they needed to make it through the month. I was so proud of that, not realizing that I was doing absolutely nothing to better our lives. I was in no condition to think. I started, once again, to drink and smoke to forget the condemning memories that kept pounding in my head. I was glad to have my children back, but I had no idea how to handle a family. Every time I decided to spend time with them, someone would pop up with a six-pack or a hit. That's right: my neighbor was on the stuff too! We lived upstairs in a duplex, and my neighbor was always knocking at my back door, trying to find a hit. This was a little frightening to me because her habit was really out of control. Sometimes I wouldn't answer the door even though I needed a fix. I thank God that my children were not old enough to know that we were in trouble. They were just happy to be with me.

Junior was three years old now, and I found myself trying to make up for the time that I lost being away from him. It was hard for me to even think about not being there when he first started to crawl, his first steps, or when he woke up crying during the night. I decided to put him in early education classes, but I found out that I could not imagine him being away from me at that age. The school informed me that there was a homeschooling available. I knew that it would be a way for me to have at least four hours a day with nothing to drink or smoke. His teacher would show up on time every day, and I was so proud on graduation day. I thought about Candace a lot.

She was still staying with my mother in Arkansas. She was going to school and seemed to be happy, but my tears continued to flow at the thought of our family being torn apart. I wanted to know what she was thinking and how she was being treated by the other children.

While I was letting my mind wander, my habit was increasing. I didn't do it intentionally, but I thought it was the only way I could forget my problems. This ten-dollar high that I thought was making me feel better was actually killing me. I felt miserable when I had to get up the next day and send my kids to school. Most of the time, I didn't even go to bed. I would hook up with my neighbor and scope out the neighborhood for drugs or go to the local bar. I felt that I had to keep my brain numb so that I wouldn't think about how messed up my life really was. Once again, I felt that I had to get away. As long as I had a mindset to return, going down south was not a problem. I did a little figuring and thinking, and shortly, we were on the bus. I was so happy to see Candace. She had grown so much. Once again, we were together.

Now I began to think about Shardee. Would it ever end? I didn't think so. I guess it was time for bad news once again. I received a phone call from friends, who informed me that my landlord thought we would not be back, so he cleaned out our apartment. I thought, this cannot be happening! Once again, I left my children to return to Milwaukee. I had used one month's rent money for our trip. People in the neighborhood had gone through the things that were left outside, so I had nothing. I stayed with my sister Chris while I waited for my next welfare check, which would be sent to the apartment. I caught the bus every day to wait for the mailman. My former neighbor and I would sit on her porch every day and drink beer and wait. We did this for a few days, and there was no check. Finally, I reported the check "lost or stolen."

A few weeks went by, and I had a visit from the county sheriff. He showed me some pictures and asked if I knew the people in them. I was shocked to see a picture of my neighbor! She had stolen my check and taken it to a bank outside of the city and tried to cash it. I guess she forgot that the bank had cameras. That was a federal offense that cost her about ten years of her life. I really felt bad for her children. She had seven children, and four of them were just babies. Eventually, I got my money back and sent for my children. Candace was with us now, and that meant the world to me.

This time I decided to stay home and really work on raising my children. I found a couple of houses, but no matter how I prayed, cried, and talked to myself, nothing seemed to work out. By this time, Grace had moved to Milwaukee. She helped me out a lot, and it got a little better. She invited me to go to church, and I felt that I had to, even though sometimes I was high. I felt bad, but for some reason, that's where I knew I needed to be. I stayed with my sister Chris until I found another house. I had even another opportunity to get back on my feet. God was always with me, and most of the time, I didn't realize it.

After that, I moved several more times, always finding myself in the same situation. Whenever I thought that we were doing okay, there I was in the same old boat. This time I found a house: a duplex again. It was okay. We lived downstairs, and the upstairs was vacant. It was as if the whole house were mine. That night, my friend and I broke the house in. The beginning of yet another nightmare! I enrolled my children into another school. By this time, getting high was really no fun. It was just a habit—and a very expensive one. Income tax time was approaching again, and I always looked forward to that time, not realizing that it could have been my last year.

Someone finally moved upstairs. I was not really surprised when I found out that she was an addict. I began to think that everyone who came around me was on the stuff, so I didn't have a chance. This was my first encounter with a real prostitute. That's when I prayed to God that I would never get to that point. She was from Chicago and had no shame. I think she was the ugliest woman I had ever met in my life (just keeping it real). I could tell that at one point in her life, she had been a Beautiful girl. I think I felt sorry for her, but her looks never stopped me from talking to her or getting high with her. Her looks never stopped her from being able to bring in more money in one night than I could have in a month. She would buy more crack than anyone could smoke in one night. Her mouth could tell the story. It actually looked like a chainsaw, but it didn't stop the men from coming to her—that was scary! Her husband and five-year-old son joined her in the apartment.

I figured that I had to stay high to live there. Days and months went past that I didn't even remember, but somehow I managed to get up to get my kids off to school. I guess I had to do that in order to have the day to myself. I began to get paranoid at this point. There was no way the police knew what I was doing in my house, but I thought they could see through the walls. I would get up on Saturday and get sober enough to go to the laundry mat. It was just on the corner from my house, and it was open all night, so we would all go together.

Sometimes Paul would go with us. He lived with us part-time. It was always a different world for that one day. We would laugh and talk and play with the kids, go out to eat, or barbeque in the backyard. These were the things I enjoyed most. Just when we would really get into that family moment, our neighbor would drop in, and sometimes even the local dope man would stop by to see if we wanted a little something to go along with our barbeque. And before I knew what had happened, I was standing there with a pipe in my hand, waiting for a high. That would quickly put an end to our family festivities.

There was a holiday coming up, and we planned to go out with a bang! I just didn't know where the bang would take me. It was late in the evening, and our boys had arrived. I found out that we had more than we could ever smoke in one night; as a matter of fact, the sight of it scared me. Yet it didn't stop me. I had smoked so much that I could hear every footstep that was made in the house. I had visions of the police outside my bedroom door. Every time the door opened, I thought they were coming in to take me to jail. Every chance I got, I would go to the other room to check on my kids. I was extremely paranoid now, and I could feel my heart getting so slow that I was about to pass out. I would stop for a few minutes and then try to smoke more. After a few hours, I didn't know how my body was going to react. My heart rate would race, and then it would slow way down. I was scared. I don't know how I found the number to the rehabilitation center at the hospital, but they came right away. Paul was trying to ask me what was wrong, but by that time, I had no words to even explain it.

When the rehab team showed up, my bags were already packed. I can't even remember how I accomplished that. My brother, Kavis, was there for a visit, and I asked him to keep the children. Thank God he was there at that time. I was in rehab for about two weeks. Paul and my brother kept the kids. I felt like a new person when I got out, and I was really happy to come home to a clean house; not only was my house clean, but my clothes were washed, and dinner was in the oven. I could hardly wait to get a home-cooked meal. Now I was ready to cash my check that had been waiting on me for a week. That's when Kavis shared another surprise with me. The landlord had showed up and informed him that they would have to get out unless she got her rent payment. She had him sign my check and give it to her. Even though I didn't abide by the law, I knew it. I immediately called the police. It was getting late in the evening when the officers showed up. Kavis told them everything. After getting his statement, they asked me to ride with them so that we could get my check back. I felt better now. It didn't take them very long to find her house. I had to wonder if this had happened before. She had a beautiful home in a beautiful neighborhood. Now I was upset again. The officer rang the doorbell, and it didn't take her very long to answer. He told her why we were there, which I'm sure she already knew and asked her for the check. She said that she had deposited it into her account. He then told her that if I didn't have my money by Monday morning, she was going to jail.

I enjoyed my weekend because I knew that Monday morning, I would have over eight hundred dollars. That Monday morning, she brought me the money and told me that she was taking me to court. I was a little nervous at first, but I was glad to get the money, and the weekend started early. First, we went to the mall, as we did every first of the month. Next, we had a barbecue; that meant there was going to be beer. Being clean and sober didn't last very long. From that point on, whenever I went to rehab, I would go right back to my habit. For me, rehab was just a time out. Eventually, we went to court, but the judge was shocked at all the illegal things that the landlord had done. She actually made me look good. I was ordered to pay her seven dollars in back rent.

After moving out of her house, I still had enough money to rent an apartment. First, I packed my things and moved them to Grace's house. We stayed with her while I looked for an apartment. Not very long after, I found a duplex apartment a few blocks away. The neighborhood seemed to be okay, and it wasn't far from the school that my kids would be attending. I knew I would love it. There was a beautiful view of the neighborhood from the balcony, and we could barbecue all year round—and that's exactly what we did.

Well, it only lasted a couple of years. Yes, after meeting the neighbors across the street and up and down the street, I found out that I was right back where I started. Everyone that I met seemed to be on the wrong track. Our landlord informed us that we had to move, but he gave me time to find something else. It took me about two weeks to find a place. We could carry most of the things to our new home. It was a three-bedroom cottage. I was glad that no one was living over or under us. We had the whole house to ourselves, including the basement. All of my children were with me at this time, and that made me feel better. The first few weeks were so scary; I don't remember ever being so jumpy. My habit was at a new level, and there was no problem getting what I wanted. The drug itself had changed. I had escalated from cocaine to crack. There were additives, such as battery acid and rat poison, and other things that could kill you right off the bat!

Whatever it took to get you hooked, that's what they used. I no longer had to cook it; it was ready and waiting. They did anything to keep you coming back. I was at the point that I stayed up for days at a time because I thought that if I fell asleep, I wouldn't wake up. Some things I can't remember even to this day.

During that time, I was able to keep my kids in school, but I was unable to attend most of their programs and parent-teacher conferences. Sometimes Junior really wanted me to attend some of his activities, and I would make myself go. And then I would Beat myself up for not going sooner. Yet sometimes I would make it an excuse to get me a drink or six! The depression was hitting me hard. Every day I would wake up wanting a drink and a cigarette, and that would lead me right back to the big stuff.

At this time, my children were able to walk to school, and they even attended an afterschool program. Now I was home by myself a lot. Well, not exactly by myself ... I always wanted to marry, but for some stupid reason, I always ended up playing house. Paul and I lived together for years, on and off, but marriage never entered the picture. Every day, I would get my children off to school and go on a mission (and it wasn't for God). My first stop would be the corner store, where I got my beer, and then I would scope out the neighborhood. I wouldn't have to look for drugs; they would find me. I decided that I could no longer wait for a check once a month because it was putting me in debt with the locals. I had to get a job. Sometimes I would walk to the lakefront for a getaway. It was always relaxing to watch the waves roll up on the Beach and the sailboat far off on the lake. And then, the dream was over, and it was time to go home. On the way back, I could only look at the restaurants, game rooms, and movie theaters, wishing I had kept the money to enjoy myself while the kids were in school. The depression I felt would give me an excuse for another drink.

One day, Paul and I walked over the bridge toward the lake. It was a beautiful day, and we decided to have breakfast. It was too bad that the only place that we could afford to go was McDonald's. Don't get me wrong: that was our favorite place to eat out at the time, but it would have been nice to try something different. We argued most of the way, and I don't even remember why. No doubt, it was about money. I filled out an application with no expectation of getting a job at that point. The manager asked if I would talk to him before I left. I could not believe he was giving me an on-the-spot interview. After only a few minutes, he informed me that the job was mine if I wanted it. I could only think that he had to be kidding! Not only did he offer me a job, but he talked about making this a career and getting my own franchise. Surely, he misunderstood something I said, or he saw something in me that I didn't see. Right then, I was just glad to have a job.

My children were happy, but my friends thought I had lost my mind. They couldn't understand why I would give up almost nine hundred dollars a month sitting at home to go to work. Of course, Paul and I celebrated that night, but I really looked forward to the next week. I was on time for work every day that I had to be there. I started off cooking breakfast (that's still my passion today). My children no longer wondered if I would cook. Whenever I came home from work, they knew I had something for everyone. The lady who trained me quickly became one of my best friends. Her name was Kathy. She promised to show me everything that she knew, and that was all I needed to know. She moved around that store as if it were made for her, and before long, I was doing the same thing.

Eventually, we began to hang out—and she could really hang! One night, I found out that she had a habit. I remember thinking that there was really no way out for me. Kathy had a habit that I could not even imagine. Any time someone had a habit bigger than mine, it was big! It scared me that she knew where to go (day or night), and we were on one every night. Yet we managed to get back to work as if nothing had ever happened. Sometimes we just stayed up all night. When I did lie down at night, I would ask God to help me. I think this is when I really began to pray because I didn't know what would happen when I went to sleep. I met more people and began to hang out more and more, but I kept right on working.

Paul and I were still together on and off, and he would get mad because I was away so much. Some of the things that went on in the streets made me run home to call him. Some people would do anything for a hit. I didn't realize that I was at the same risk as the ones who were doing some of any and everything.

Getting married right then seemed like a dream that I once wanted to come true, but now I didn't have time to think about it. I never wanted to have lots of men, so to help prevent that, I kept in mind that I could catch something and die a slow, painful death; and I hate pain! It was crazy the way I was thinking sometimes, but it kept me alive in many situations. Don't get me wrong: I was in danger many times, playing games that could have easily taken me out. But I was only trying to stay afloat without selling myself, which I witnessed so much of every day. I felt myself pushed to that point sometimes, but I would cry and pray every step of the way ... that is, whenever I had a chance to stop and think about it.

▪Chapter 9

My children were really growing up now. They were real troopers—survivors. They had to be. They would always try to help other children in the neighborhood. I can't remember one time, living on the east side of Milwaukee, that they didn't bring someone home to eat, spend the night, or just hang out until we could find their parents. During my addiction, I helped a lot of people, but I couldn't help myself. While I was in my own world, Buffum Street was getting really bad. Different people were moving in and out, so every few months, we had to get to know new neighbors. I still had a desire to make it better for my children, so we would barbecue a lot. They loved to do that. One of my neighbors would always want to join in so that we could keep our children's attention off what we were doing. We would always start the party just drinking and cooking while the children played in the bedroom.

One day, I had just checked on the children when I saw my neighbor's eighteen-year-old daughter come in and lock the front door behind her. She ran right past me to the back. As I walked back toward the kitchen, I heard a loud noise at the door. When I looked back, I saw the door fall in. Police were everywhere! Two of the officers ran to the back bedroom. They caught one of the locals selling drugs out of the window. Our kids were in the next room, playing games, and some of them began to cry. One police officer told us to get on the floor. One said, "Get your hands up," and another was telling us not to move. Trisha, my neighbor, was just about drunk. She began to argue with one of the officers because she did not want to get on the floor. Why? Because she still had beer left! I just knew we would all get shot. At this point, I thought someone was going to die. Especially when I realized that one of them was a dirty cop. Not to my surprise, about three of them were. The only thing on my mind was getting out of there. The children were still crying, so I asked one of the officers if I could take them to my house next door. Surprisingly, he went for it. All they really wanted were the drugs and money. We watched them leave, and no one was arrested. We were just glad to be alive, and no one even brought it up again. The drug dealers were right back on their posts to recover their loss.

I had to take a small break every now and then, and I would always go to church. Through all of this, I was still working, and now I was a manager. My daughter, Candace, was working with me at McDonald's during the summer. She was a hard worker at fifteen years old. I give her props for being at work when all of her friends were enjoying their summer. Eventually, the lakefront changed, and McDonald's changed ownership. Our whole crew was laid off. I received unemployment for a while, but that left me with too much time on my hands and no money in my pocket. It seemed as though everyone in the neighborhood was sitting out on their porches with nothing to do. One day, we were sitting outside drinking, and a van passed by. I couldn't believe my eyes; my son Yheme was blowing the horn and waving to make sure I saw him. I looked inside my can of beer and looked up again. It was really him! Later, he informed me that he had been driving for a "minute" (that meant a long time). He was only eleven or twelve at that time.

I decided that things had to change; I just had no idea what to do. I worked a couple of temporary jobs. They were all great jobs that could have taken me straight to the top, but I wouldn't have been able to party like I wanted to. Paul and I were having our differences at this time, and I felt that I had to do something different. Time went on, and whenever he felt as though he needed a break from whatever he was doing, he would leave and come back whenever he wanted, and I let him do this to me. That was a dangerous lifestyle, and I knew that I deserved better. It was as though my brain just did not function.

I finally found a job that I could stay with; it was probably because my unemployment was running out, but the job was really okay. It was a large factory. It was a mile or two from my house, and I could ride the bus. I worked in packaging. Sometimes I had to work nights. When the buses stopped running, I would walk home. That meant I needed a car. The man at the corner store informed me that he had a car for sale. Things were looking up. He was always good to my children and me. I decided to take a look at the car. It was a clean, shiny, black Buick. It was a family car, and I did have a big family, so I made arrangements to buy it. No more walking home from work, at least not for a while.

I still partied a lot. Walking forty or fifty blocks to a party that I really wanted to go to was not an option. Now I was able to drive to the other side of town. Sometimes I would wake up and run to the front door to see if my car was outside because I couldn't remember driving home the night before. It happened a few times before I realized that I could have been dead. The drinking and driving didn't stop because I thought I could handle it. Yheme would always stay up to make sure I made it home. I somehow managed to keep a job. There were always those days when

I barely made it through the door before I collapsed in my recliner. I'll never forget one day I was so tired, and as soon as I sat down and closed my eyes, Yheme came in and asked me for the keys to get a movie out of the trunk of the car. I'm not sure how much time had gone by when I decided to go and check on him. As I got up out of the chair, I heard a crash. I ran out to the street and saw my shiny new car was wrapped around a tree! I don't know exactly what I did, but I know the whole neighborhood heard me. And I still got a ticket for the tree!

Now I was back on the bus. I really missed my car, and I knew that I had to find a way to get another one. Not long after that, I found a better paying job. It was a factory job, and we made big, iron hangers that came in all different colors. I was a machine operator, and the pay was great. There were only two women in the whole factory, so the men really spoiled us. I even tried not to stay up too late when I had to go to work the next day. It was very seldom that I succeeded in doing so, but I tried. One day, I was really tired, and I should have called in, but I had to have the extra money. Everything was going okay until I started to let my mind wander and got my thumb caught in the iron-bending machine. My first reaction was to pull, which we had been told many times not to do. I looked at the girl next to me in a panic, not even realizing the top of my thumb was hanging. Someone had called the ambulance, but my boss would not wait. He decided that it would be faster to use his truck. It was though every stop sign and red light was invisible. I was so scared that we were going to have an accident, I almost forgot about my thumb. But I was quickly reminded of it when I saw the needle that the doctor was about to use. He gave me eight shots around the base of my thumb to deaden it. I didn't feel anything else, even when I watched them sew it back on. The insurance on the job paid for almost everything, even therapy. They really wanted me to stay, but when my thumb was healed, I didn't even consider staying. I regretted it later.

There I was, on the unemployment once again. I started to get so drunk and high that I would fall on my knees beside my bed, crying and praying for God to help me out of the trap I was in. Sometimes I would fall asleep on my knees, but the next day I would find myself standing in front of the liquor store, waiting for it to open. Paul and I were together again (if that's what you want to call it). He was working at the time, so he would stay with me a couple of weeks and then go back to his sister's house.

One day my friend, Kathy, came over to let me know that my boss from McDonald's had been looking for me. She informed me that he was managing another store on the other side of town, and he wanted me to work for him. This was a miracle! The next day, I went to fill out an application and was hired on the spot. I started out as a crew chief, and then assistant manager, and before I knew it, I was manager once again! This job was about four miles from my house, so I had to have a ride. Before long, I was able to buy a minivan. It really felt good not to have to catch the bus that far. I still had a really bad habit at this point, so I know someone had to be praying for me because I was handling thousands of dollars every day, even when I didn't have a dime in my pocket. If my boss had known who he was trusting with all of that money, he probably wouldn't have called me back to work.

Paul and I were still playing house, and it was all good—so I thought. One Monday morning, as he was about to leave for work, he said that he would see me on Saturday. I laughed and kept doing whatever I was doing at the time. He stopped and repeated himself, and everything was quiet for a moment. The next thing he said sent chills down my spine. "She doesn't like it when I'm gone too long," he said as he walked out the door. Yes, that's how he let me know he was seeing someone else, even though I had known about it for some time. Things in my life were getting pretty bad, and I knew it was because of my habit. Surely he didn't think I would willingly share my man with another woman! Just as I was about to really lose it, I felt as though something was holding me.

He walked out the door, and I just slammed it behind him. I mumbled to myself, "Okay, I'll see you later." I could see him looking back as he headed to the car. I think he expected me to follow him and really show out, and so did I. As I watched the car pull off, tears began to flow with no effort on my part. There was something in my gut telling me that it was over for good. I went to work in a daze. That day went by so fast. Before I left, I told my boss that I would be moving down south. I really don't remember why I told him that I was leaving, but he was a great guy, and he listened to every lie I must have told him. I asked him if he would write me a letter of recommendation for McDonald's back home. He said it was short notice, but he would do it. He didn't want me to leave, because he trusted me to do my job, and I don't remember ever letting him down.

When I got off work, I went to look for Kathy. We talked about some things that were going on, and then we just took a ride around town. Tears started to flow again. I turned on the radio and realized it was on a gospel station. A very familiar song was playing: "Open up My

Heart." As I listened to the words that she was singing, it seemed to touch the innermost parts of my heart. It really broke me. I told Kathy that I was moving back down south. I don't think she paid me much attention at that time. She was hoping I was just going through a phase. She kept telling me that everything would be okay, yet she seemed to agree with just about everything I said. I couldn't believe it was Thursday already. I stayed high every day after work. It was always early in the morning before I decided if I was going to sleep.

I told my children on Wednesday to let their teachers know that we were moving on Friday. I was in no condition to talk to their teachers. By Thursday night, most of their friends knew that we were leaving. They thought I would change my mind until they saw the U-Haul attached to my van. Of course, I had no money to get a U-Haul, but after explaining my situation to my children's mentor, Jody, she helped me with everything that I needed. I would not forget to thank God. Until then, I often wondered if God was anywhere around after all the things I had done. I hated to see my children so upset, but I knew there was no turning back now. They were all teens, except for Junior. He was twelve. They said I was taking them away from the only friends they had. This was true, but it wouldn't change my mind. The next day, they went to their school for the last time to say goodbye. There was almost complete silence as we loaded the U-Haul. Some of their friends were there to help. We loaded up and were on our way. I could hear my kids crying and mumbling until they fell asleep. My niece, Felicia, and her newborn baby, Trevion, were with us. It would be a little over nine hundred miles to get to town, and I was the only driver. So, while everyone slept, I poured coffee inside me to stay awake. We stopped in Chicago so that my uncle Leon could make sure we got on the right road. I didn't know how I would make it without a hit. I kept thinking, *If I could drink one beer, everything would be okay,* but I knew that wasn't going to happen.

When we got to my mom's house, I was so full of coffee that I could hardly blink. But I was home. I didn't want to live in Arkansas, but I knew that I would be there for a while until I knew what we were going to do. My children were so mad at me for taking them away from their home that it was hard to get them to see that things would eventually get better. My boys were adapting; on the other hand, my girls were having a few problems getting used to the idea. They simply refused to make any new friends or even go outside after school. Candace had lived down south for a while, yet she had problems coping with the idea of leaving Milwaukee. She was in high school now, and that made a big difference.

My nerves were a mess! I immediately got in contact with someone who could fix me up. And then I decided to go back to work. I know that was a little backward, but that's what drugs will do for you. I started to work, even though the money was nowhere near what I was used to, but it was shocking how the south had become so educated on drugs. It was almost a little Milwaukee. I wanted out, and now, I thought I would be in this situation for the rest of my life. Everything I needed was now right within reach, and I took advantage of it all. I had visions of my grandchildren being ashamed of me. Of course, at that time, I didn't even have any grandchildren. It was a nightmare because every time I decided, "This is it," someone would show up with a tester, and I was always the first one to test it out. The dealer wouldn't take my money at that point because he knew he would get it later. I had a spot where I usually hung out every day. It was getting bad, but I held on to my job.

My mom and dad moved out of the family house and rented a house so that we would have a place to stay. They were great parents. And to think, I know I brought them so much embarrassment. After they moved, I began to go home drunk, which I never did when they were there. Once, I came home early in the morning. I was so drunk and high that I could hardly get to the bed. I knew that it was almost time for my children to go to school, so I just laid there. Suddenly, I was having a hard time catching my breath, and as I thought about getting up, I felt my heart stop Beating. That's right: my heart stopped Beating! I began to pray to God. It was weird, as though I was thinking a prayer. I was asking God to just let me see my children grow up. I also prayed for an opportunity to see my grandchildren. I didn't want to die alone. I even thought about going to hell and burning forever. It seemed as though I had been there forever when it had only been a few minutes. Then, all of a sudden, I sat up, and I felt my heart Beating again. I was so scared, and now I was sober.

I got up and walked through the house for a moment, whispering to God, thanking him that he had answered me. I knew that it was almost time for my children to go to school, so I went back to bed and just laid there until I heard them get up. Did that stop me from partying? No! I didn't tell anyone about it at that time because I knew they would think I was crazy. When the children were off to school, I was right back at the spot, not even remembering what I had gone through. While sitting at the table, smoking and getting high, my cousin and I would occasionally discuss the Bible and how we would someday go to church. We would eventually start to cry. Sad to say, it didn't stop me from doing what I was doing; as a matter of fact, it got worse because I couldn't figure out how to stop. I actually felt as though I was losing my mind.

Walking the streets looking for my next high seemed to be a regular part of my life. Working at McDonald's down south was no longer supporting my habit, so I had to have another job. I had always said that I would never work at a production factory, but I found myself headed that way. I knew that I would have to give up the drugs in order to pass the drug test, and that was a job in itself. I applied for the job and waited.

▪Chapter 10

Meanwhile, Felicia had found an apartment, and I went to visit her. She lived behind a church that I remembered from when I was a child. We were so close that I could hear the preacher. When I realized that he was someone I knew growing up, I made plans to visit.

A couple of weeks had passed before my new job called me. I was so glad to get the job because I had worked so hard to stay clean, even though I was still drinking every day. The cocaine was out of my system, but not out of my mind. I had said to myself that I would have one blast after I got my first check, and that would be it! The first week, I did a little something, but I was frantic that someone would find out and it would cost me my job. Even though I was scared, payday was coming, and I started to make plans. I had almost stopped smoking cigarettes (maybe a couple a day), but I was still drinking and getting high. My supplier wouldn't turn me down, knowing that I was working at the factory. We would get paid on Thursday, and I could hardly wait. Now it was Sunday, and I decided to go to church. I took Junior with me in the hope that I wouldn't be as nervous. Not only did I remember the pastor, but his wife as well. I didn't remember ever hearing that they were married, but I could tell that they were meant for each other.

I had a hard time listening to the preacher because I really wanted a drink. I could not get used to the liquor stores closing on Sunday, and I couldn't find a bootlegger that morning. We went inside and sat on the backbench by the door that was reserved for the ushers. For some reason, I was really nervous and couldn't get that beer off my mind. I wanted to lose myself in the crowd. As I looked around, I realized that it wasn't a lot of people, but I could feel love from them. I don't remember the whole sermon because my mind just wouldn't stop wandering. I didn't miss the part about love and forgiveness; and when he asked if anyone wanted to give their life to God, I found myself walking to the front of the church. Once again, I asked God to help me. I really hoped that he would be there one more time. I wanted that change so badly. It was as though something inside of me held me hostage, and I couldn't break free. As the pastor prayed for me, I could feel the presence of God. I knew that feeling from years ago at my church in the country. Tears began to flow uncontrollably from my eyes, and I knew that it was done. God had forgiven me, and I felt the love of God! I was free! At that time, I found out that you don't always have to fall down. That was one thing I thought would happen when you receive the Spirit of God. Even though I didn't fall down, I knew it was done. When I left the church, I told everyone who would listen what had happened to me. When I got home, I called my mom and told her everything. She was so happy. And then, I called my cousin who had partied with me, faithfully, almost every night since I had returned home. Of course, at that time, she didn't want to hear that I wasn't coming back to the table. I don't think she even believed me at that point.

When I went back to work, I felt good. I didn't have to pretend anymore. Ever since the day I asked God to forgive me, my life has changed. I haven't smoked cigarettes, haven't drank, and the most amazing thing—the habit I had for years, the drugs—I don't want them anymore! The taste was gone! I had heard of people quitting, eventually, but from the day I walked out of that church, I felt like a new person. I didn't want any of those things that kept me hostage. People said it couldn't be done, and I believed them, but once I believed God, he changed my life. Even my suppliers knew something had happened to me. My neighbor, Patricia, was very shocked. I know she was happy for me, but it meant that we would not be sharing cigarettes or just hanging out as much. I could tell that she was a little disappointed. She would come over sometimes, but I think she was just checking to see if this had really happened to me because this was a miracle! Her mother was a member of the church, so she was very much aware of what I was talking about. Even though she laughed and talked with me, she didn't stay very long, because my conversation had changed. One day, Patricia began to tell me how much she wanted to stop smoking. I was so happy! She even started to go to church.

Shortly after that, we moved into our own house, and my children were glad that things were changing. They often told me how things had changed for the better. There were still some issues in my life, but for some reason, they didn't seem to bother me anymore. All I could think about was the fact that I had a fresh start. I could breathe better, and everything around me was much brighter. I started to read my Bible and attend Bible study and Sunday school so that I could understand some of the things I was reading about. I really enjoyed attending this church because the pastor was a great preacher and teacher. He would explain things so that I could understand. I don't like it when I have to go to the dictionary to understand what someone is trying to tell me. It was the love of my pastor, his wife, and the members of the church that made me want to stay there. They didn't condemn me for the things I had done, but they loved me in spite of everything I had done in the past. I eventually got my missionary license and was really excited about the Word of God.

There had been a major change in my life. It wasn't perfect, but I was loving it. I went to the store one day, and on the way back, I noticed flashing lights behind me. I was about a half-block from my house, but I decided to pull over, knowing that I had done nothing wrong. I gave the officer my license and waited patiently. When he returned to my vehicle, he asked me to get out. He said that he had a warrant for my arrest. I started to ask God what was going on. I had given my life to God and asked him to forgive me for my sins. This could not be happening to me! The officer did not handcuff me, but he put me in his car, and we proceeded to go downtown. I couldn't believe they had my van towed! I began to wonder if this was "you reap what you sow" time. I was taken to the police station, where I was sure they would realize that it was all a mistake, and they would let me go. They told me that I had a fine that had not been paid. I tried to explain that I had paid everything at the prosecuting attorney's office. Evidently, my payment was late, so it wasn't cleared before the warrant had gone out. It was the weekend, so they were having a hard time getting in touch with the prosecutor. While I was waiting, a sheriff showed up and said that he was there to transport me to the county jail. He seemed to be a nice man so somehow, I thought if I explained what had happened, he would just let me go—not! Once again, I was not handcuffed. I sat in the front seat with him. He was on the phone, trying to get in touch with the prosecuting attorney. I talked to him about the church: the change God had made in my life and the fact that I had just received my missionary's license a week ago. The entire time, he was on the phone to no avail. He took me several miles outside of the city, where there was another car waiting for me. It was about to get scary.

There were two officers in an unmarked car waiting to take me the rest of the way to the county jail. I was waiting for him to handcuff me, but the sheriff opened the back door, and as I got in, he said goodbye. The other officers didn't say very much; they just had casual conversation amongst themselves until we got to the county jail. I thought about all of the things I had done, and this was my first time going to jail. I knew I could not take back the things I had done, but I knew I loved God, and he loved me. I couldn't help thinking there was another reason for my being there. The time had come for me to be booked. Now I was nervous! Throughout the whole process, the lady kept apologizing for what she was doing. Now it was time to go to my cell. I once again thought about the change God had made in my life, and I knew I wasn't alone. I just couldn't figure out why I was there. They gave me a mat to take to my cell, and it was really hard to carry. As I walked down the hall, someone walked behind me and said, "Here, let me carry that for you." I still have no idea who that young man was. We entered a room where people were playing cards, talking, and seemed to be having a good time. I looked upstairs by the tiny cells and saw my cousin Paula. She was shocked to see me there. So, I came to a conclusion that she was my purpose for being there. I had to be there to talk to her about changing her life. I quickly realized that was not the reason. She was not interested in anything I had to say. I started to pray again because it was getting late, and I just wanted to go home now. I went into my cell, put the mat on the floor, and just sat there, staring at nothing. Just as I was about to prepare to stay for the night, I heard a shallow voice say, "You're the one I've been waiting on."

It was the lady in the bunk. She struggled as she turned to face me. When I saw her face, I realized I knew her from the streets. She told me who she was and why she was there, but I could tell that she was sick, and it kept her from saying everything she wanted to say. I told her some of the things that I had gone through and how God had changed my life. She was a much older lady, and I could tell that the drugs were taking a toll on her. We talked for a while, and she said that she was glad that I was there, but she needed to rest. Before she went to sleep, she said that she would come to visit our church when she got out. Just as we finished talking, I heard my name over the intercom. They told me I could get my things together and go. I quickly realized that the lady was the reason that I was there. I came out to find my mother and cousin Edith waiting. I told them what happened, and we talked and praised God all the way home.

A few weeks after I got out, I began to look for the lady. She was only in for a minor charge, so she should have been out. Every time I went to church, I looked for her to walk through the door, but she never came. She had told me that she lived in a mobile home not far from the church. I began to ask about her because I never saw anyone there. My brother told me that she had died not long after she got out of jail. I went home and cried because I wanted her to come to church and experience the same thing that had happened to me. All of a sudden, I felt a sense of peace, and I thanked God that I had an opportunity to talk to her in her last days, in hope that one day I will see her again.

This is just a skip through my life. I know that lots of people have bad habits and think that they are better off than the crack addict—not true. We have to realize that all bad habits are bad, and one is no better than the other. You have to love yourself enough to want what God wants for you, and that is to live an abundant life. I am not saying that I am perfect, but I do strive for perfection. Even though I am still learning, I will continue to tell others about the goodness of God because I can truly say, "I am not ashamed of the gospel of Christ." I've been at death's door several times. I never want anyone to go through the hurt and pain that I have experienced. But if you are going through some things, and you feel there's no way out, just start reading the Word of God and find a church that is teaching the Word. It is important that you understand what you are reading. God is so real, and it's a shame that we can believe the weatherman, the newspaper, and even our enemies when it comes to heeding the cause, but we can't believe God! It is my prayer that everyone who reads this book, who does not know God, will have an encounter with him and find true peace and happiness.